BIRDS OF A FEATHER

BY Marjorie S. Hancock

This book was written and photographed by me to bring information about all kinds of birds to my grandchildren Ben, Lindsay and Aliza.

As we continually displace our wild life by abusing our open space we are losing our natural beauty. We need to pay more attention to those whose habitats we are destroying. We must speak for the ones who cannot speak for themselves

TABLE OF CONTENTS

IBIS   PAGE 8-9
PELICAN   PAGE 10-11
THE SNOWY EGRET   PAGE 12-13
GULLS   PAGE 14-15
SKIMMERS   PAGE 16-17
CORMORANTS   PAGE 18-19
GREAT BLUE HERON   PAGE 20-21

ANHINGA   PAGE 22-23
FLAMINGO   PAGE 24-25
SANDPIPER   PAGE 26-27
SPOONBILL   PAGE 28-29
WOODSTORK   PAGE 30-31
FRIGATEBIRD   PAGE 32-33
DUCKS   PAGE 34-35
AMERICAN EAGLE   PAGE 36-37
OWL   PAGE 38-39

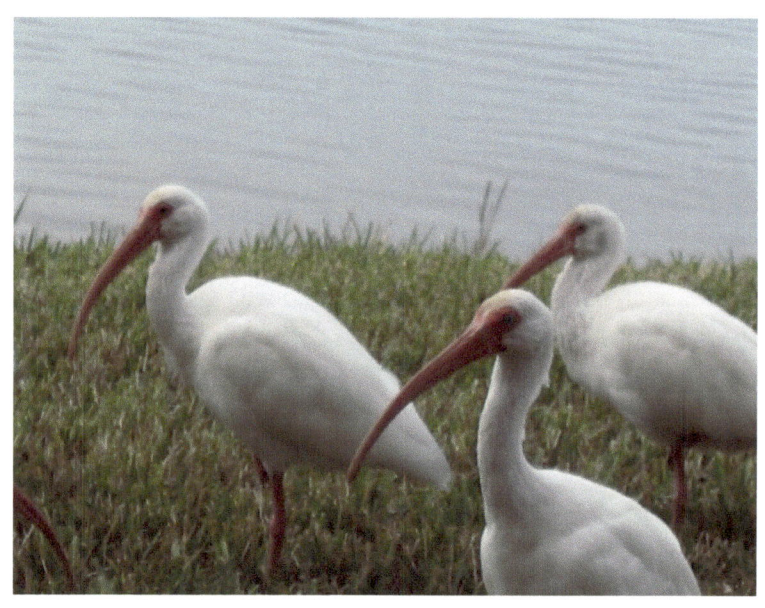

IBIS

Three little Ibis walking down the street
One named Alice one named Pete
The third named Susie, so cute and sweet
I have an idea said Alice to Pete
Let us go to the lake and get a treat
So off they flew leaving Susie behind
Sitting in the grass a tear in her eye
Wait said Pete we forgot our sister
That makes us a nasty miss and mister
So back they went to get little Susie
Because a family is always kind to each other

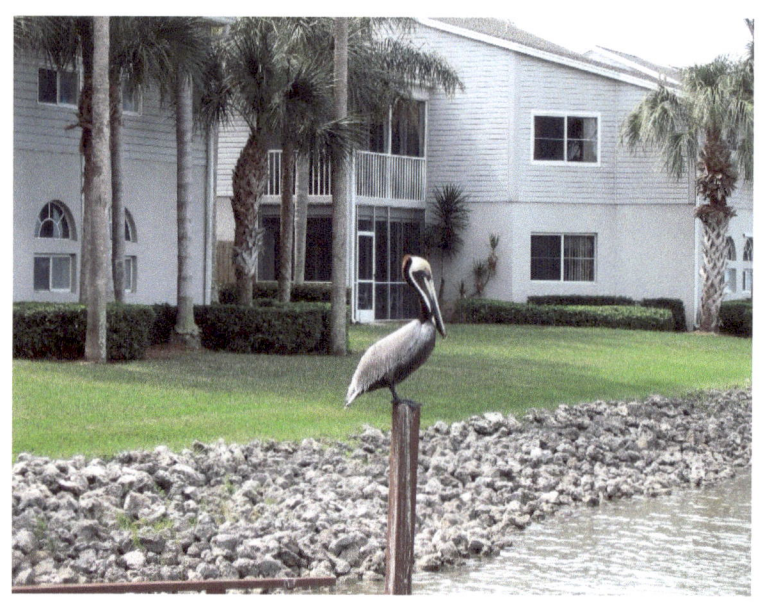

PELICAN

Po Po the pelican was flying over the bay
When all of a sudden he saw what you may
Call a belly full of mackerel down in the water
He took a big dive and went splat on the sea
He took a big gulp and what did he get
But a glob of water and no fish for his dinner
His big old belly was still very hungry
So he decided that another dive was in order

This time success was the thing
He grabbed a fish and started to sing
Here is my supper and his tail did a wiggle
It went back and forth which meant he had his dinner

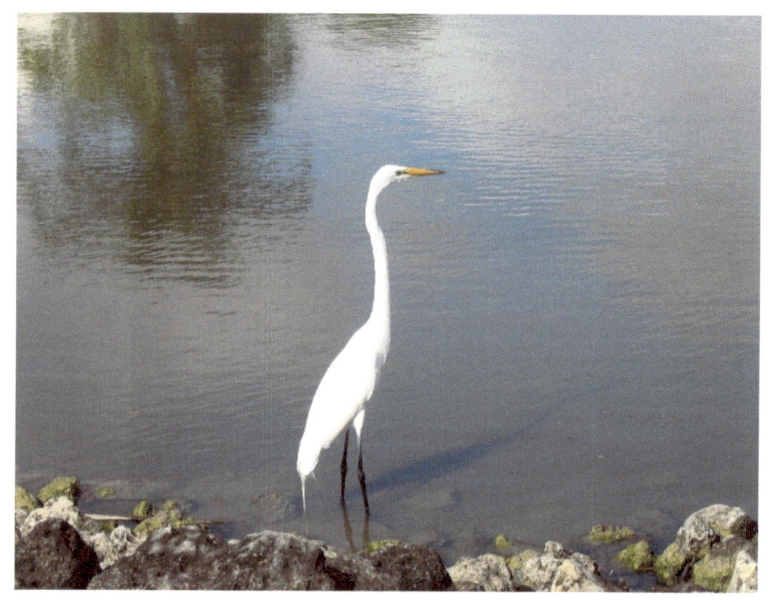

THE SNOWY EGRET

Sally the Snowy Egret sits on the dock
Her beautiful white plumage, which she wears as a frock
She has no regrets for the lovely life she leads
She lives on fish like the rest of the flock

She races down the beach with her quick little steps
To stir up the fish as she takes little nips
She gets real hungry and feels a growl in her tummy
For the lip smacking mackerel that is so yummy

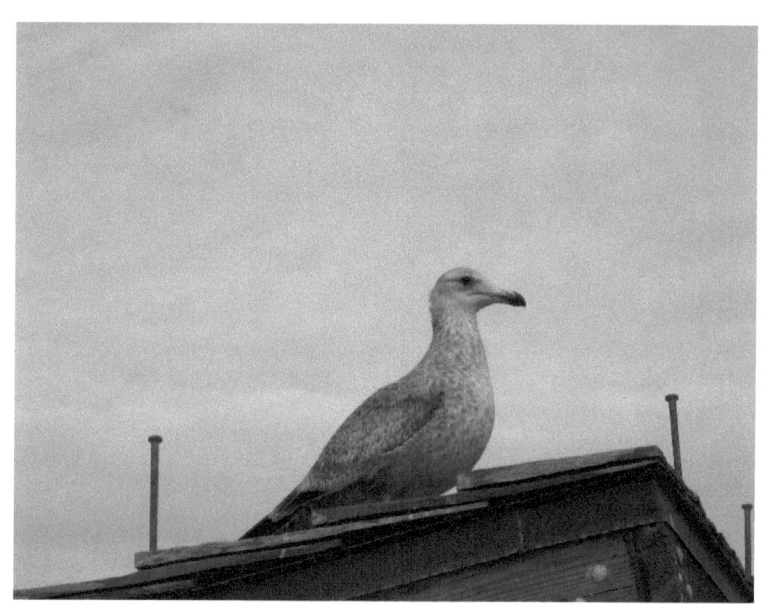

GULLS

The Laughing Gull we all know well
They fill the skies from beach to dell
Gulls soar and laugh so loud
We often have to yell
To hear the stories we tell

When we set on the beach we have to be careful
They swoop and fly down to the table
So guard your cookies and sandwiches well
Because the busy gulls are not a fairy tale

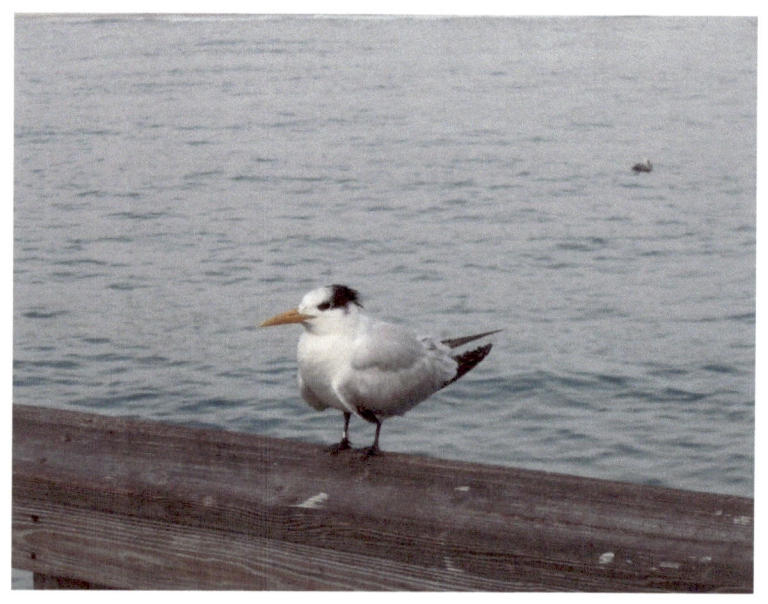

SKIMMERS

Skimmers are so cute with their long lower beak
Have a fishing skill that can not be beat
They fly close to the water in a V formation
A skill to be envied by all creation

They skim along the bays and beaches
Looking for seafood and fish that is so delicious
They rake the water with their over sized bills
When full they fly into the wind with never a spill

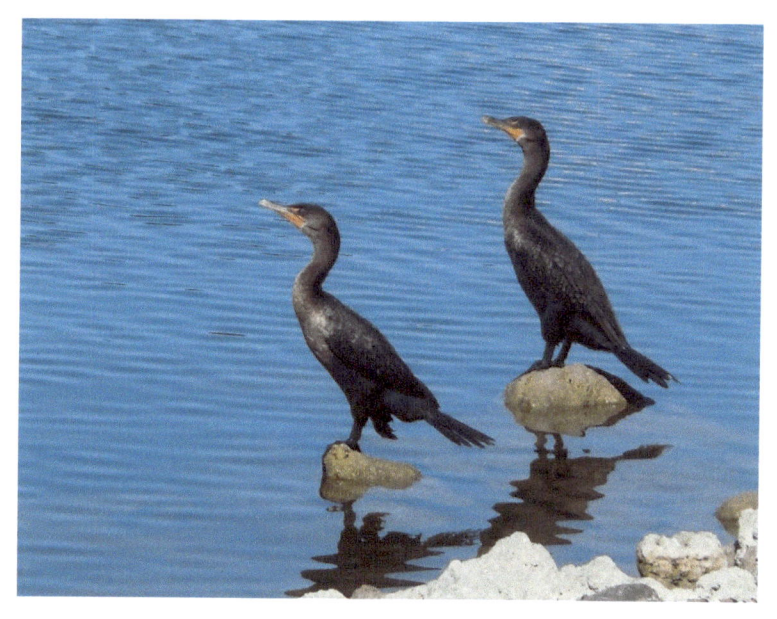

CORMORANTS

Coco the cormorant has a hook on his beak
He floats on the water and looks so sleek
His beak is perfect for grasping a fish
Then after dinner he sits by the creek

He sits in the sun to dry his feathers
He is glad he is free to enjoy the weather
And not have to work like his captive relatives
In Florida waters he is free to be clever

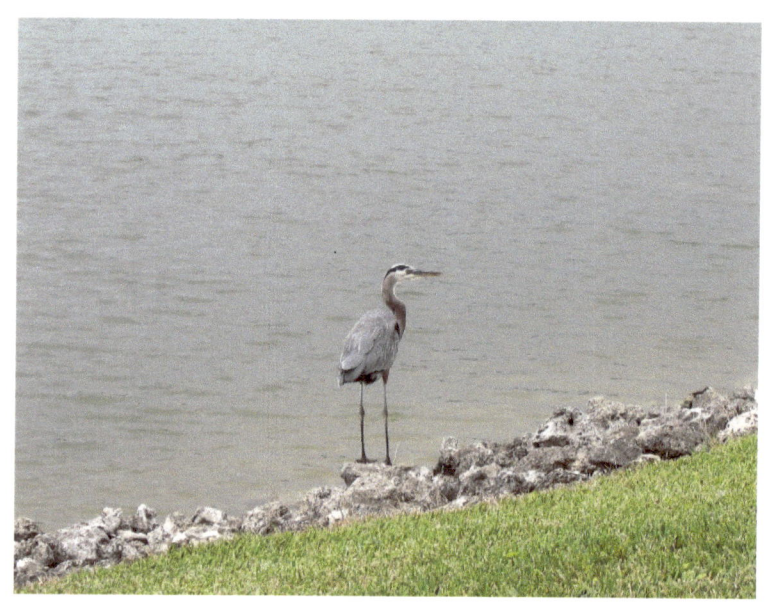

GREAT BLUE HERON

Howie the Great Blue Heron is a beautiful sight
So stately and demur in demeanor and might
When he walks down the shore with feathers galore
He is the envy of those who wish they had more

With the pretty blue color and long legs and neck
There is no mystery to what bird name to pick
He likes to fish for food in swallow water
And takes off in flight he is such a graceful fellow

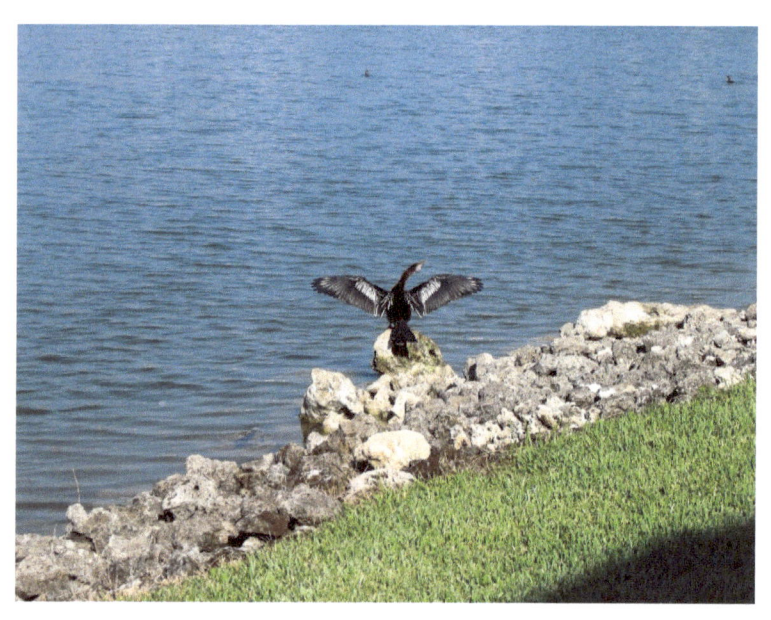

ANHINGA

Minga the Anhinga decided to go for a refreshing swim
You could only see his head and neck that appear quite thin
An illusion soon to be dispelled
When from the water he did rise on a whim
To our surprise he is chubby not slim

He stands on the dock post to get himself dry
Because it if he is wet it is very hard to fly
He has no oil glands for waterproofing his feathers
So sun himself he must so he can soar in all weather

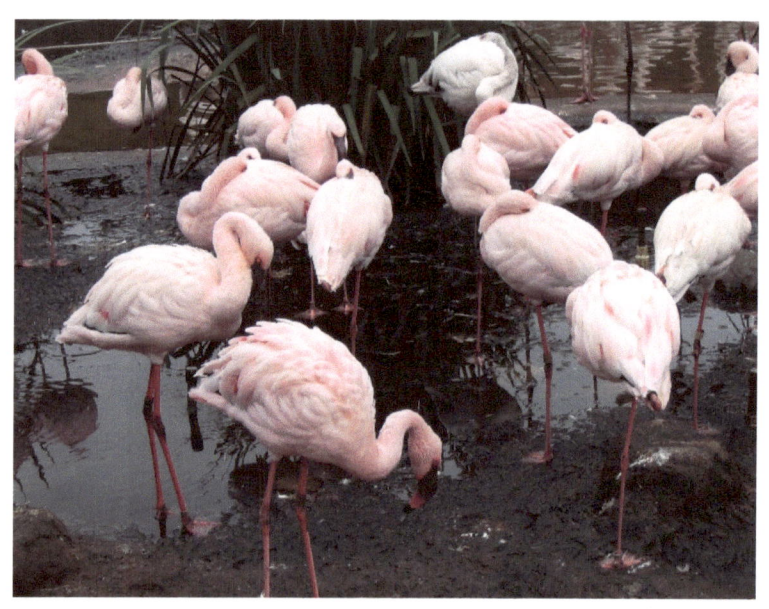

FLAMINGO

Frances the beautiful bright pink flamingo
Is so tall and gorgeous she makes your heart sing
As on one leg she stands as she looks in the water
Then all at once she catches a fish, bingo

She can remain nice and tall as she gathers her hull
Of food that she wants with no need for the mall
Her beak has a bend with a unique angle
So she can gobble her food still have a mango

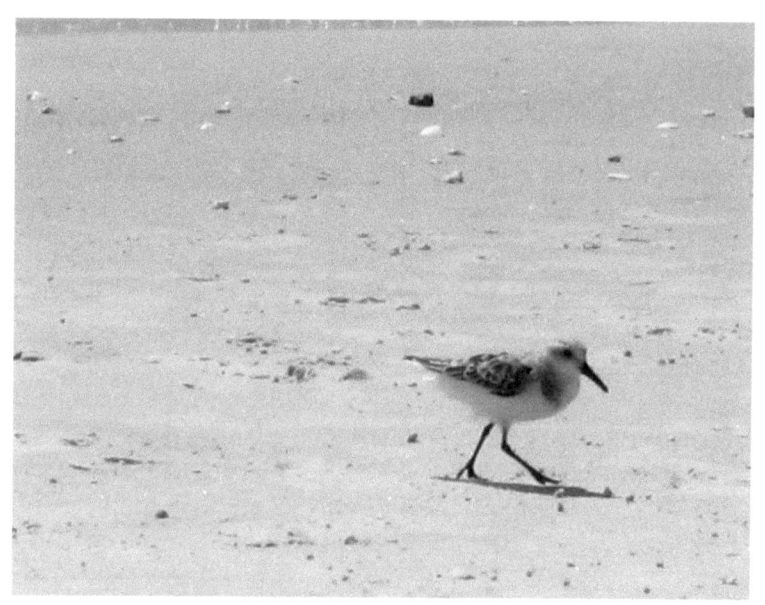

SANDPIPER

Sandpiper's come in a variety of names the willet, sanderling and dowitcher for a few
They race down the beach in such a hurry you would think they had a curfew
They come from the Artic in the spring and fly on down the coast in spite of the rain
We are happy they are here so cute and small they always look new to us all

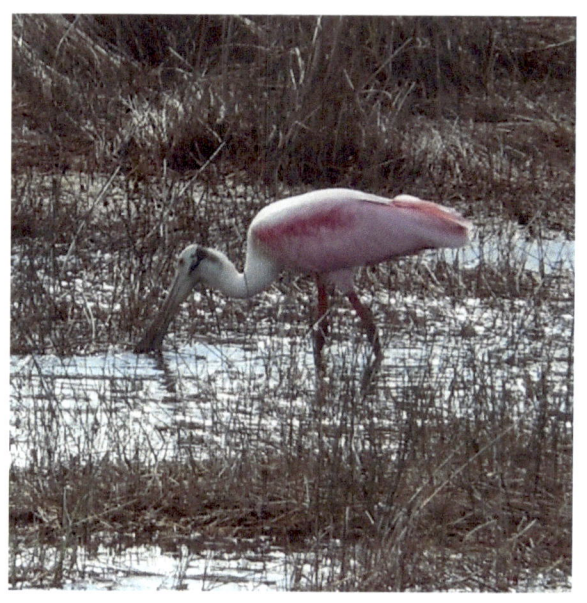

SPOONBILL

The pretty pink Spoonbills are quite unique
They look like a Flamingo but are rather neat
Their bills are the shape of a large flat spoon
And their red eyes make them look like a goon

When the spoonbills walk through the water
They swing their beaks back and forth to the fish it's a startle
Then all at once the beak goes shut
But they never catch anything as big as a skunk

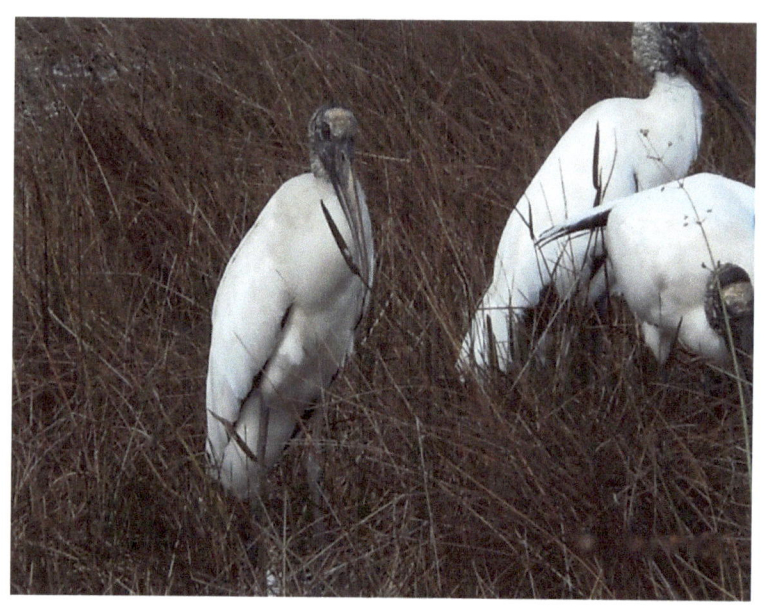

WOOD STORK

The Wood Stork is a very social fellow
He like to fish and nest in a manner that is so mellow
When he fishes his beak moves faster than the other birds
Then his stand so stately they call him the Preacher bird

He flies with such grace up in the sky
His wings out stretched in black and white
His bald head and iron colored beak
Make you wonder if you are looking at a streak

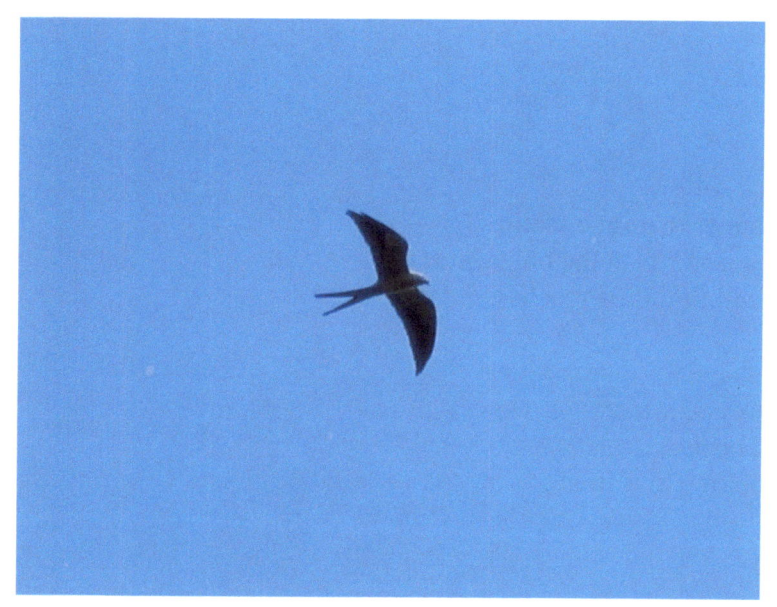

FRIGATEBIRD

The wonderful Frigate bird had a huge wingspan
She will soar in the air and fish where she can
Her nice name the Pirate may be over used
As he usually catches his own food with a giant swoop

As you spot her in the sky her tail has a fork
When she sits in a tree her head and neck are dark
She likes to depart from very tall trees
Otherwise with such big wings she might hit her knees

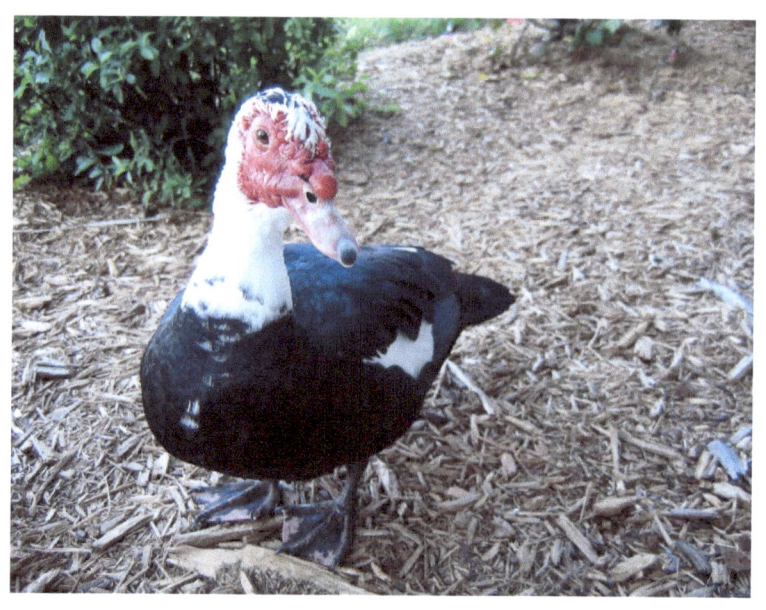

DUCKS

The very familiar Mallard duck we all know so well
Seems happy to land in a body of water the size of a pail
The green headed male is known as the drake
And his lady partner is a hen make no mistake

The Muscovy is a relative but looks very different
Her face is all covered with fleshy duck matter
They live at the beach and on every lake
And if you drop any food it is theirs to take

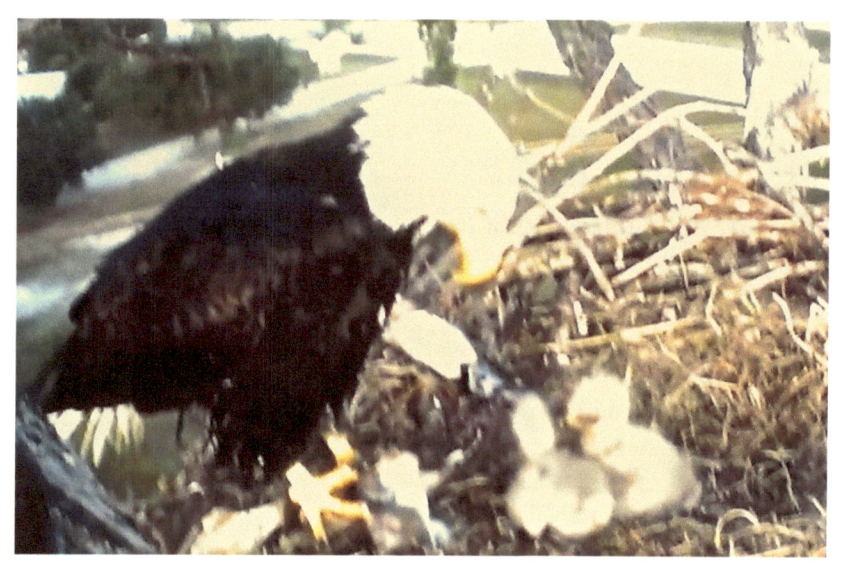

AMERICAN EAGLE

The grand American Bald Eagle is our symbol of freedom
He is not really bald his head is covered with white feathers
He can soar in the heavens and search for this dinner
When he spots his next meal he is sure to be a winner

The eagle lives in the same nest year after year
He continues to make additions with out any fear
The Bald Eagle is no longer endangered species
But we must be vigilant so the eagles do not parish

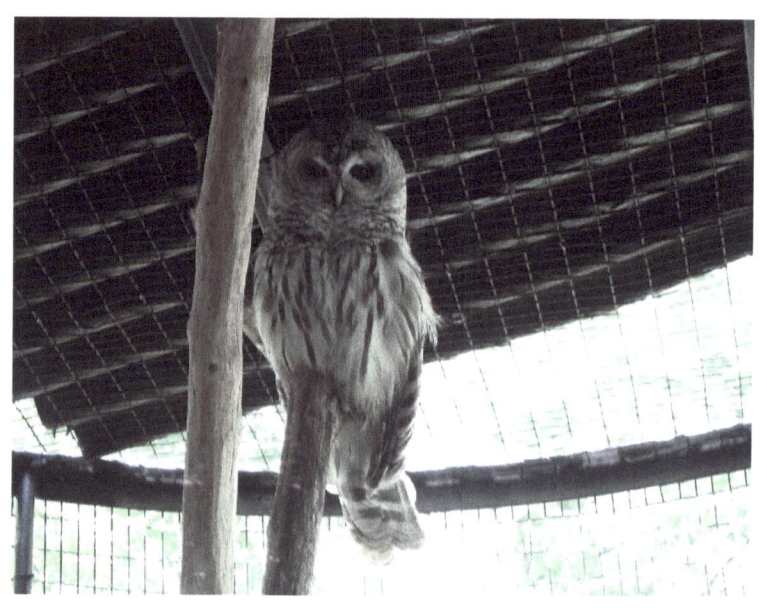

OWL

I must leave you now with the wise old owl
He sits on his perch asleep all day
I guess he dreams of dark scary night
The "who" that he screeches gives you a fright

The owl's great big eyes help them to see better in the dark
They are great hunters and never confuse their dinner with tree bark
Their ears give them keen sense of hearing which is bad for their prey
So they hunt at night and sleep all day

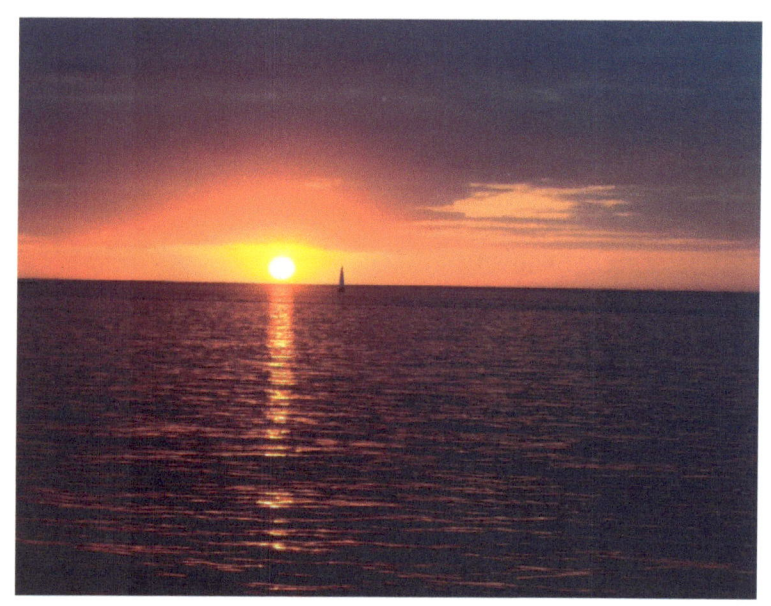

THE END

ISBN-13: 978-1518654008

www.ingramcontent.com/pod-product-compliance
Lightning Source LLC
Chambersburg PA
CBHW050904180526
45159CB00007B/2789